THE APPRAISAL OF MANAGERIAL PERFORMANCE

Arthur Meidan

AMA Management Briefing

amacom
A DIVISION OF AMERICAN MANAGEMENT ASSOCIATIONS

Library of Congress Cataloging in Publication Data

Meidan, Arthur, 1936-
 The appraisal of managerial performance.

 (AMA management briefing)
 Bibliography: p.
 1. Executives—Rating of. I. Title. II. Series.
 HF5549.5.R3M38   658.4'07125   81-19061
 ISBN 0-8144-2271-3   AACR2

©1981 AMACOM
A division of American Management Associations, New York. All rights reserved. Printed in the United States of America.

This Management Briefing has been distributed to all members of the American Management Associations. A limited supply of extra copies is available at $5.00 a copy for AMA members, $7.50 for nonmembers.

This publication may not be reproduced, stored in a retrieval system, or transmitted in whole or in part, in any form or by any means, electronic, mechanical, photocopying, recording, or otherwise, without the prior written permission of AMACOM, 135 West 50th Street, New York, N.Y. 10020.

First Printing

About the Author

Dr. Arthur Meidan is senior lecturer in management (a rank parallel to that of associate professor in the United States) and director of the MBA program at Sheffield University, England. He has spent over 15 years in management, including three years as consultant to the United Nations Industrial Development Organization (UNIDO). He is the author of over 30 papers and monographs on business policy and marketing management, a member of the editorial board of the *Quarterly Review of Marketing,* and associate editor of the *Journal of Enterprise Management,* published by Pergamon Press. He has lectured and consulted widely on management and performance appraisal in Europe, the Middle East, and South America.

Dr. Meidan earned his bachelor's degree in economics and his MBA from the Hebrew University, Jerusalem, and his Ph.D. from the Bradford University Management Center, England. The author may currently be contacted at Sheffield University, Sheffield, England. Tel. 0742-661064.

Contents

1 Introduction   7
2 Finding the Right Criteria for Assessing Performance   14
3 Methods of Appraisal   23
4 Utility as a Measure of Performance   37
5 Appraisal in Functional, Divisional, and Matrix Organizations   43
6 Issues Arising from Current Appraisal Practices   48
7 Appraisal of Performance and Effectiveness   53
8 Summary   56
Bibliography   59

1

Introduction

When you get right down to it, almost everyone with a stake in an organization has a hand in the performance appraisal of its managers. Stockholders, for example, appraise managerial competence on the basis of the organization's dividend payout and the price appreciation of its securities. Unions judge it in terms of wage levels, job opportunities, and stability of employment. Consumers, suppliers, and creditors size up competence against such criteria as the value of the organization's product or service, the promptness of its payments, and its adherence to contract terms. Finally, the community at large makes its decision on the basis of the organization's public responsibility.

But performance appraisal *within* the organization itself is generally acknowledged as one of the weakest points in organizational development. Indeed, organizations have been so weak in this regard that the appraisal of executive performance—or lack of it—has been referred to as the "Achilles' heel" of management development. Only recently have we begun to develop accurate ways of finding out whether practicing managers are really competent in their jobs.

Performance appraisal is, of course, absolutely necessary if an organization is to prosper in the highly competitive world of modern business. Measuring the performance of managers provides an organization with information necessary for the success of its administration (in the short run) and its business policy (in the long run). This information can reveal both the strengths and weaknesses of an organization, and indicate where reorganization, planning, training, and/or recruitment are needed.

Much of an organization's ability to achieve its objectives stems directly from the competence of its managers. And if managerial competence is so crucial for a corporation's success, stability, and survival, we can, with good reason, wonder why adequate appraisal systems have not evolved long before now. The truth of the matter is that development has stalled because of two factors:

- Failure to look closely at the reality of management roles as they differ from one organization to another—and to search for systems that take this diversity into account.
- The tendency to apply static appraisal methods that focus on the past, rather than on the dynamic relationships between present and future.

This management briefing is a quest to identify those appraisal systems that link a diversity of roles and relationships to what we might term "organizational utility." In simpler words, we want to know which appraisal systems are best for which organizations, given the realities at hand.

The quest is by no means simple, because the concept of utility (what is truly fitting and useful) is by no means a constant. It varies with the type of company and its organizational structure, with levels of management within a company, with changes in the environment over time, and from culture to culture.

Consider, for example, what happened following the 1973 Middle East War, when the Arabs reacted in a way that had significant effects on the economic environment in the West. Before 1973, the criterion of achievement in business was growth; in less than a decade, it shifted to getting the maximum yield from resources. "Productivity" is our new utility, and one of the criteria applied in performance appraisal may well deal with a manager's ability to get the most from his or her resources.

The cultural variations can be just as pronounced: In the 1960s, when interest in appraisal was at its highest in the West, progressive

Japanese firms installed systems of appraisal that emphasized merit, performance, and ability. But the firms tended to ignore the outcomes of these appraisals because the results conflicted with the heavy traditional emphasis on formal education, seniority, and expressed loyalty to the organization.

It's clearly beyond the scope of our present publication to chase down all of the global and cultural variables that affect appraisal. We can, however, begin to grasp other key variables, such as the diversity of management roles and the objectives of appraisal as they differ among types of organizations.

DEFINING "MANAGER"

The species that goes by the title "manager" has such diverse characteristics that we often wonder whom and what we're talking about. We could (and sometimes do) sit for days theorizing about the question. But from a practical point of view, it's not too difficult to arrive at a definition.

For example, the old, theoretical idea of a manager being someone who is responsible for the work of others is not wholly accurate. There are individuals on management teams who are essentially professional experts and who contribute to the organization, but who have little to do with the work of others. Equally inaccurate is the notion that managers are the people who perform management tasks: setting objectives, organizing, implementing, delegating, and so on. This ignores an important fact: Not all people who carry out these functions are considered managers.

In practice, though, managers—like army officers—are so simply by definition. Chaplains and doctors in the army are commissioned officers, even though their functions are decidedly nonmilitary. The same holds true for senior staff members who may prefer to think of themselves as professionals rather than as managers.

The point is this: Rather than spend a great deal of effort trying to refine our definitions of "officer" or "manager," let's simply accept the fact that the person *is* what the title says. This is a first step toward confronting the reality of diverse roles we spoke of earlier.

KNOW THE OBJECTIVES

In dealing with this diversity of managers, it's wise to have specific objectives to steer the appraisal process. But recognize that appropriate objectives, like the concept of organizational utility, vary from one situation to another.

Generally speaking, the objectives of managerial appraisal are: (1) to evaluate performers or improve performance in order to make promotion/dismissal/transfer decisions, review salaries, and identify training needs; (2) to allocate financial, production, technical, and marketing resources; (3) to aid in business planning; and (4) to make possible changes in organization and control systems.

Most appraisals are intended to serve more than one purpose. For example, at General Electric in the mid-1960s the avowed purpose was both to justify salary action and to motivate performance—at least, that was the original intent. As it turned out, the salary decision crowded out the motivational aspects from the minds of both the appraisers and those being appraised.

In profit-making organizations, profit will usually be the dominant criterion, even for service departments. In nonprofit organizations, profit as such is not applicable, and the more general term "contribution to organizational utility" can be substituted. Implicit in this is the assumption that the organization has a corporate identity and is capable of having corporate objectives, and is not merely a coalition of interests.

How does profit tie in with the appraisal of managers? Perhaps this will become somewhat clearer if we consider the two distinct kinds of profit:

- Earned profit, which is earned by sound management planning and control and by efficient executive action—in other words, earned profit stems from successful strategic and operating management.
- Windfall profit, which is the result of very large, seemingly unpredictable changes in the environment.

As far as windfall profits are concerned, you can argue that the highest function of management is to *foresee*. Thus, in assessing the very highest grades of manager, windfall profits and losses should be taken into consideration, even though they may seem to be unpredictable.

The relationship between profit and performance appraisal becomes even clearer when we begin to take managerial rank into account.

MANAGEMENT LEVEL MAKES A DIFFERENCE

The purposes of appraisal may also depend upon the rank of the manager and the type of organization. The higher the rank of the manager and the greater the manager's degree of autonomy, the more the emphasis will be on his or her performance as a *strategic manager* over long time spans. The lower the rank, the more the emphasis will shift to his or her performance as an *operational manager* over shorter periods of time.

As a general rule, the higher the manager's grade, the fewer criteria there are by which to evaluate performance (see Exhibit 1). Toward the top of the organizational hierarchy, we have those managers whose success or failure is identifiable with the success or failure of the autonomous organizational units themselves. In a profit-making organization, we're talking, for example, about a divisional general manager. In nonprofit organizations, we're thinking of a director of education, a chief of police, a director of research, and so on. These are the managers who rule the organization. They might be evaluated on the basis of a single criterion such as divisional residual income (total profits less notional interest paid on capital employed).

At the other extreme of the hierarchy, we find those junior managers who implement multiple objectives laid down by others. We tend to evaluate their performance on more diverse factors: a profile indicating strengths and weaknesses.

Between the two extremes we find the semiautonomous managers who work *within* plans generated by their superiors in the hierarchy. These are the persons who run the organization. Typically, they work with job descriptions defining their function, responsibility, and authority, and perhaps with objectives set by their superiors or with detailed budgets specifying their required contribution to the overall corporate plan.

Exhibit 1. How criteria and time spans for appraisal differ for various management levels.

Type of Manager	Scope	Function	Criterion of Performance	Time Span of Appraisal
Great	Autonomous	Total environmental predicting	Single measure	Indefinite
Big	Semi-autonomous	Strategic	Few measures	Several years
Middle-junior	Non-autonomous	Operational	Profile	Yearly

Unlike the assessment of the "ruling bosses," which is often an ad hoc business because of the time span of their activities (among other things), assessment of the "running bosses" tends to be a routine task for higher management. The most popular method of appraising these semiautonomous managers is management by objectives (MBO). The essence of MBO is that the manager draws up his or her own job description and sets his or her own performance goals. But this last requirement is clearly unreasonable to the point of absurdity for most managers in complex organizations.

POST-MORTEMS ARE INADEQUATE

Most organizations employ some sort of system of appraising the performance of their managers. Most of these methods, however, are static in that they are largely concerned with how the manager has performed in the past and concentrate on only one—or, at most, a few—aspects of management. But managing is a dynamic process concerned with the present and the future, and the appraisal process should employ standards that reflect this. It is this need for appropriate methods that has led us to the brink of developing new systems—systems that take into consideration the different aspects and elements of a manager's job.

By now, it should be apparent that as we step closer to that brink we confront a complex set of relationships. The chapters that follow are structured to help organizations sort through that complexity in order to identify and implement appraisal systems appropriate to their identity, their objectives.

One can grasp a significant part of the content simply by thumbing through and studying the exhibits. In most cases, the exhibit takes the form of a matrix. These plot various approaches to management appraisal against a large number of variables: type of organization, level of management, organizational structure, and so on. In fact, such browsing provides an accessible method for previewing the book.

But the exhibits tell only part of the story. It's equally important to catch the logic that makes one system of appraisal better than another for any given situation. The next chapter starts us off by looking at the criteria for assessing performance.

2

Finding the Right Criteria for Assessing Performance

Those of you who followed Alice in her adventures through Wonderland will recall the travesty of justice depicted in the closing episodes. The king, acting as judge, hopelessly muddles the jury by using the words "important" and "unimportant" interchangeably, then calls for the verdict before the evidence is presented. This satire is, of course, a far cry from what usually happens in the process of managerial appraisal. But the passage does underscore an important point: Without a workable set of criteria, we have no way of knowing which evidence is important and which isn't.

Generally speaking, three sets of criteria are used for evaluating managerial performance:

1. *Inputs*—the performance of managerial activities.
2. *Outputs*—the results achieved.
3. *Personal qualities*—personality traits of the managers being assessed.

Inputs become appropriate where managers have little autonomy, but follow established procedures; and when counseling, transfer, training needs, decisions, and human inventory compilation become important.

Outputs are important in all of the above situations; however, they become most appropriate when dealing with managers who have a high degree of autonomy and where the decision is to promote, demote, or terminate employment.

ACCOMPLISHMENTS ADD UP

Measuring outputs is a relatively easy task in profit-making organizations (especially manufacturing firms). Sales, net profits, production figures, and so on are all units of objective measurement than can be used to evaluate performance. Some outputs in nonprofit organizations are easily measured, too: the percentage of crimes solved (in a police department); the annual death rate per 100,000 population (in the public-health sector), and average reading scores (in the schools), to name but a few. Other outputs in nonprofit organizations are not so easily measured, however. For example, how does one measure ethnic attitudes toward the police, the quality of subclinical health, or the social skills of students?

Personal traits criteria are usually not very objective. These judgments may be thinly disguised as quantitative behavioral statements ("is imaginative . . . has been observed to produce a large number of original ideas"). They may be disguised assessments of outputs ("articulate and personable" for a person in a public relations function). Or they may be relevant assessments of how the manager affects other people's outputs.

APPRAISAL IN PROFIT-MAKING ORGANIZATIONS

The most generally accepted criteria for assessing managerial performance in profit-making organizations is profitability. This sounds fairly clear-cut; however, in practice the calculation of profit bristles with accounting difficulties, involving problems like overhead, depreciation, and evaluation of inventories. Further questions arise: Should we look at profit *before* or *after* taxes, and in relation to what? Very probably, profit before tax is the better indicator of managerial performance. After all, why should the vagaries of government fiscal policies figure in the assessment process?

Profit before tax related to assets employed is one commonly used financial ratio by which the overall performance of a unit and its autonomous manager can be judged. This ratio by itself is often of limited use, but it can be compared with the ratios of similar firms.

Besides the overall return on investment ratio

$$\frac{\text{profit before tax}}{\text{assets employed}}$$

other more analytical ratios can be compared. For example:

$$\frac{\text{Profit before tax}}{\text{Sales}}$$

$$\frac{\text{Production costs of sales}}{\text{Sales}}$$

$$\frac{\text{Sales at cost}}{\text{Average stocks}}$$

$$\frac{\text{Sales}}{\text{Assets employed}}$$

$$\frac{\text{Marketing and distribution costs of sales}}{\text{Sales}}$$

$$\frac{\text{Average of outstanding debt}}{\text{Average sales per day}}$$

There is, unfortunately, one serious drawback to using any of these financial ratios: The behavior of the manager may be adversely affected in response to the criterion selected. For example, if a manager is judged on absolute profit, he or she may be motivated to maximize profit by the prodigal use of capital. This may be against the interest of the organization, since the opportunity cost of capital could be higher than the return on marginal projects. Similarly, if a manager is judged on return on investment (ROI), he or she may be motivated to undertake only those projects with the greatest ROI and ignore less profitable ones that might increase total profit but bring the ROI down. Again, this may be contrary to the interest of the organization.

The criterion that, to a very large extent, avoids these undesirable behavioral consequences is the maximization of residual income. Essentially, residual income equals profit *less* the cost of capital employed. Confronted with this criterion, the manager is given the incentive to expand, employing capital up to the point at which the marginal return on capital equals its marginal cost, thus maximizing the net absolute.

Where the manager is not totally autonomous, as in the case of a divisional general manager, the criterion has to be qualified. A manager cannot be held responsible for decisions taken over his or her head. For example, if the manager is not authorized to dispose of unwanted assets, he or she should not be held responsible for the interest charges against them. And if uneconomic transfer prices between divisions, decided upon by top management, reduce divisional profits, some adjustment should be made. Therefore, a fairer criterion would be: Controllable residual income equals controllable profit less interest on controllable capital.

However, even this criterion needs to be qualified. It is essentially short-term, and an unscrupulous divisional general manager moving through the organization might maximize the firm's short-term residual income by neglecting expenditures on medium- to long-term innovation (R & D for example). DuPont guards against this by not putting the cost of a development into the investment base of a division or subdivision until the new product has been put on the market.

General Electric, on the other hand, identifies eight key areas in which continued failure would prevent managerial success. These are: (1) profitability (residual income); (2) productivity (output per unit of input); (3) market position; (4) product leadership; (5) personnel development; (6) employee attitudes; (7) social and public responsibility; and (8) balance between short-run and long-run goals.

The introduction of a further range of criteria presents problems. Quite possibly, some of these criteria are unnecessary, since, in the final analysis, they are so closely linked with profitability as to be subsumed by it.

One problem that must be faced in using the eight key areas mentioned above is that of quantifying performance. Data based on one or more of the following four criteria—profitability, productivity, market position, and personnel performance—are relatively easy to obtain, largely objective, easily quantifiable, and therefore generally practical (see Exhibit 2).

Criteria such as leadership, employee attitudes, social and public responsibility, and balance between long- and short-term goals, however, are difficult to quantify since the data base is subjective (Exhibit 3). Any appraisal based on these areas, therefore, is usually difficult.

APPRAISAL IN NONPROFIT ORGANIZATIONS

The appraisal of an autonomous or semi-autonomous manager of a nonprofit organization, providing goods and/or services, presents no new problem in principle. Even though profit does not enter the picture, such considerations as financial break-even, reduction of subsidies, and maximizing the funds available on a fixed budget may be objectives.

Other objectives, such as productivity, product leadership, and market position, may or may not apply. The quantification of these objectives presents about the same degree of difficulty as in profit-making organizations.

Although nonprofit organizations offer a wide variety of goods and services, they can be said to fall into five basic categories:

1. Organizations that provide services (or goods) for which there are no close substitutes, and which customers may purchase if they wish.
2. Organizations, funded by public authorities or by donations, that provide consumers with services they are at liberty to use or not use as they wish; for example, public libraries, museums.
3. Organizations, funded by public authorities, that operate as monopolies and provide goods and services that are essential or quasi-essential; for example, garbage collection, water supply. Also, organizations that provide services that in civilized countries one cannot avoid accepting; for example, police and street lighting departments.
4. Organizations that provide goods or services purchased by the

consumer for which there are close substitutes; for example, bus services, electric utilities.
5. Organizations whose principal objective is to survive in order to influence people, expand membership, or make ideological statements; for example, churches, political parties.

The criteria by which the performance of managers of these organizations can be judged may be classified in a number of ways. One possible way is suggested below, with indications of quantitative or quasi-quantitative measures that could be used by particular organizations:

1. *Financial*

    Break-even over the reasonable long term if the organization is intended to be self-supporting; for example, electric utilities.

    Satisfactory output measured against financial input if the organization is publicly funded; for example, areas and population policed, students taught at college, patients treated, money earned and saved by work in a commune.

2. *People Reached*

    Market share for the boards of nationalized companies.

    Number of visitors to museums and theaters; membership of churches and political parties.

3. *Product or Service Excellence*

    Purity of water for a water department; freedom from breakdown in garbage collection; punctuality of trains and buses.

    Critical acclaim for theaters and national standing of museums. Crime rates, losses due to crime, percentage of crimes solved by the police.

4. *Public Satisfaction with Services*

    Subjective measures obtained from surveys in which satisfaction/dissatisfaction with the police, local schools, street lighting, and so forth, can be measured on a seven-point semantic differential scale.

Exhibit 2. Quantifiable criteria for appraising managerial performance in profit-oriented organizations.

Key Areas for Assessing Performance	Ease of Quantification — Conceptual	Ease of Quantification — Practical	Objectivity/ Subjectivity	Technique	Typical Quantitative Measures
1. Profitability	Easy	Laborious but routine	Objective but some judgment involved	Routine accounting data collection and analysis	1. Net profit 2. ROI (return on investment) 3. Residual income
2. Productivity	Easy	Laborious but routine	Largely objective	Routine management accounting	1. Output per hour 2. Output per machine month 3. Output per fixed capital 4. Yield of finished product per unit input of raw material 5. Total productivity index
3. Market position	Fairly easy	Laborious but often routine with some ad hoc investigations	Objective (once definitions are decided on)	Sales figures, trade association (and similar) reports, and market research	1. Absolute sales 2. Trends 3. Market share 4. Numbers and size of competitors
4. Product leadership	Not easy	Not easy	Mainly judgmental	Internal executive panel Market research	1. Ordinal ranking of product quality with competitors 2. Ordinal ranking of value of product/service range 3. Consumer satisfaction

Exhibit 3. Major nonquantifiable criteria for assessing managerial performance.

Main Criteria for Assessing Managerial Performance	Ease of Quantification — Conceptual	Ease of Quantification — Practical	Objectivity/ Subjectivity	Technique	Typical Measures of Analysis
1. Personnel performance	Easy	Fairly easy	Mixture of objective data and subjective judgment	Human resource accounting techniques Personnel department's staff inventory	1. Percentage of appropriately qualified staff at all grades 2. Percentage upgrading of qualifications 3. Percentage of promotables 4. Percentage ranked "better than average" or above
2. Employee attitudes	Rather difficult	Not easy	Mixture of objective and subjective	Pooling executive opinion Personnel department records Questionnaires	1. Nominal ranking by executives of staff satisfied or dissatisfied 2. Percentage man hours lost through disputes 3. Absences and punctuality 4. Numbers using grievance procedure 5. Labor turnover rates 6. Employees expressed attitudes on scaled questionnaire

The Appraisal of Managerial Performance—21

Exhibit 3. Continued

Main Criteria for Assessing Managerial Performance	Ease of Quantification		Objectivity/ Subjectivity	Technique	Typical Measures of Analysis
	Conceptual	Practical			
3. Social and public responsibility	Extremely difficult	Extremely difficult	Mixture of objective and subjective	Accident statistics	Percent of staff days off as result of accident or work-induced illnesses
				Damages awarded by courts	
				Favorable /unfavorable mentions in in media.	Damages awarded
					Numbers of each kind of mention weighted by importance
				Analysis of firm's costs	
					Percent of costs employed in offsetting social costs
				Environmental indices	
					Donations
					Measures of pollution, leadership in pension schemes, etc.
4. Balance between long and short run goals	Extremely difficult	Extremely difficult	Mainly highly subjective	Pooling executive opinion	Percent of manager's time spent on long-and short-term goals
				Managers' diaries	
				Observers' questionnaires	

22—AMA Management Briefing

3

Methods of Appraisal

Perhaps a dozen or so methods for appraising managerial performance are currently available. They can be grouped in six major categories: (1) comparative procedures, (2) absolute standards, (3) direct index, (4) field review technique, (5) feedback of appraisal interview, and (6) performance statistics methods. The six categories are summarized in Exhibit 4.

Broadly speaking, the first four categories attempt to highlight a manager's activities during a specified period of time. In a sense, they are post-mortems of a manager's activities in one or a few specified areas.

The techniques used in the last two categories relate appraisal to a much broader view of management, and the managerial function is seen as an ongoing process that links the past with both the present and the future. These approaches view performance appraisal as part and parcel of the entire managerial process, and they extend the scope of the appraisal to include virtually all of the basic elements of managing: organization, planning, delegation, control, review, motivation, development, and communication. These methods aim at improving the whole managerial process, as well the performance of each individual manager, on a year-round rather than a year-end basis.

COMPARATIVE PROCEDURES

There is nothing complex about the comparative procedures approach to managerial performance appraisal. Managers are simply compared with one another on any characteristic or activity that is of interest to the appraiser. The appraisal is made on the basis of one dimension that seeks to ascertain the manager's overall effectiveness in the organization. There are two basic ways of carrying out a comparative procedure: the ranking technique and the forced distribution method.

The Ranking Technique

This technique can be subdivided into three distinct approaches: straight ranking, alternative ranking, and paired comparisons. In straight ranking, managers are evaluated in comparison with others holding similar positions within the organization. The procedure consists of asking the appraiser to consider all managers holding the same rank and identify the best performer, the second best, and so on down to the very poorest.

Alternative ranking is similar to straight ranking, except that the evaluator is first given a list of all the managers, then asked to identify the best and poorest managers and remove their names from the list. The evaluator continues removing the managers in pairs until the very last pair is reached.

Paired comparisons is another variation on straight ranking. Here, the appraiser compares and ranks each manager with every other manager. The better manager will be determined by the number of times he or she is chosen over other managers. In general, the number of comparisons can be calculated using the formula $\frac{N(N-1)}{2}$, where N denotes the number of managers to be ranked.

The chief advantage of the ranking technique is its simplicity. All the evaluator has to do is arrange the managers in order, from best to poorest. This is also a natural technique, because such ranking takes place in everyday life. Since the evaluator is forced to appraise all managers within a specified period of time, the method is subject to less inter-individual, constant error such as leniency, central tendency, and strictness. One further advantage is that ranking procedures between different rankers are almost always agreeable. This is especially true for the alternative ranking method.

Exhibit 4. Managerial performance appraisal methods.

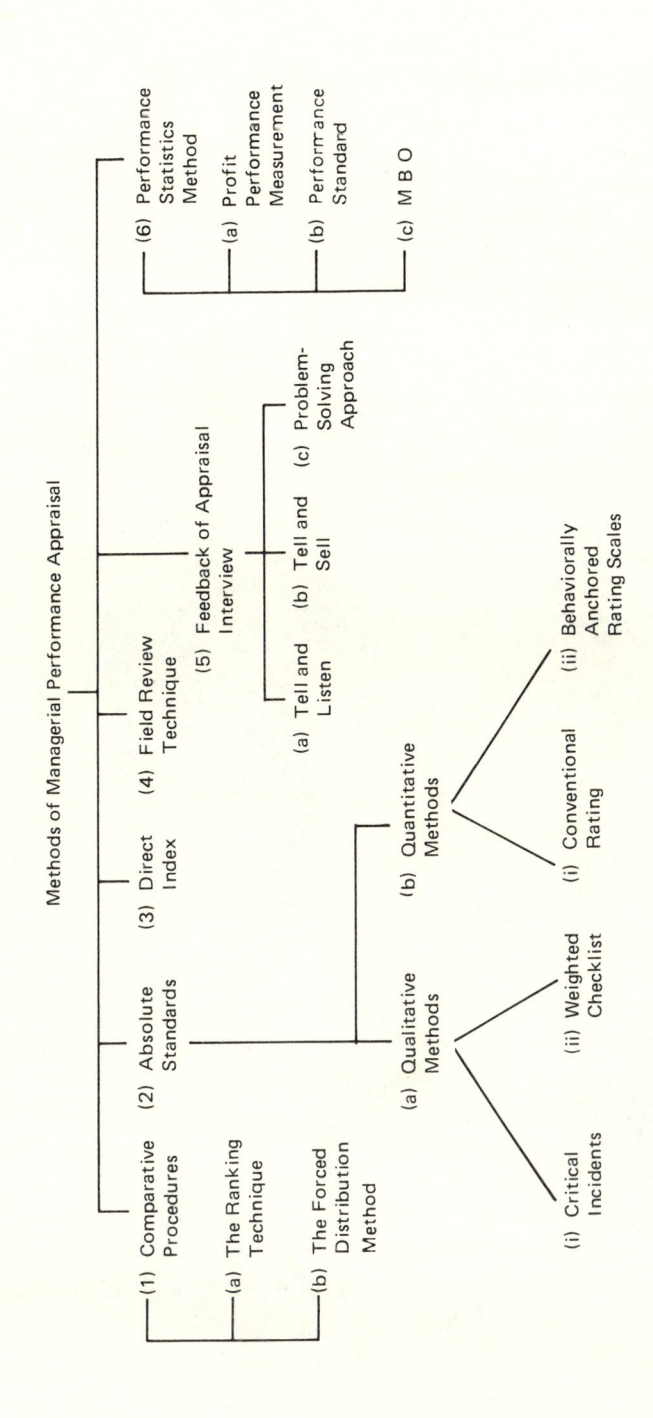

Methods of Managerial Performance Appraisal

- (1) Comparative Procedures
  - (a) The Ranking Technique
  - (b) The Forced Distribution Method
- (2) Absolute Standards
  - (a) Qualitative Methods
    - (i) Critical Incidents
    - (ii) Weighted Checklist
  - (b) Quantitative Methods
    - (i) Conventional Rating
    - (iii) Behaviorally Anchored Rating Scales
- (3) Direct Index
- (4) Field Review Technique
- (5) Feedback of Appraisal Interview
  - (a) Tell and Listen
  - (b) Tell and Sell
  - (c) Problem-Solving Approach
- (6) Performance Statistics Method
  - (a) Profit Performance Measurement
  - (b) Performance Standard
  - (c) M B O

There are, however, four major limitations to the ranking technique. First, managers are ranked on only one dimension, which means that a manager who did not perform very well in the dimension used for ranking, but did very well in other dimensions, would be ranked unfairly. This limitation makes ranking a highly unrealistic method. Second, if the number of managers to be ranked exceeds ten, then ranking by paired comparisons becomes difficult. Third, the magnitude of the differences between successive ranks may not be the same, so that, for example, the difference between the third and fourth individuals may not be equal to the difference between the fourth and fifth individuals. Finally, it is difficult to apply the results of ranking for developmental and feedback purposes, simply because the method provides little by way of insight or information.

The Forced Distribution Method

Here, the evaluator is forced to rate managers on the basis of a normal distribution curve. For example, the evaluator may be required to rate 25 percent of the managers "above average," 50 percent "average," and 25 percent "below average." One major advantage of this method is that it can include comparisons on several performance factors, rather than just one dimension, as is the case with ranking.

ABSOLUTE STANDARD TECHNIQUES

In this technique, individual performance is compared against some set of absolute standards. This method makes it possible to evaluate managers on several performance criteria, rather than one characteristic. In general, this method can be subclassified into two groups: qualitative methods and quantitative methods.

Qualitative Methods

These methods require the evaluator to decide whether statements in a prepared checklist apply or do not apply to the manager being appraised. This can be done in two ways: the critical incidents method and the weighted checklist technique.

In the critical incidents method, a checklist of critical incidents judged to be important in carrying out a manager's job is drawn up for each manager. The evaluator—who is normally the manager's superior—is then required to rate the manager against the checklist. Needless to say, great care must be taken in drawing up the checklist, since the selection of statements is crucial to the success of this method. Also, there is a possible drawback in that the method implicitly assumes that the many factors affecting or contributing to performance can be condensed into a relatively few sentences from which measurements are made. Nevertheless, this technique can serve as a basis for managerial developmental actions, as well as for evaluation purposes.

The weighted checklist technique, on the other hand, requires first that a weighted checklist containing a number of statements about the manager's performance on the job be drawn up by someone with considerable expertise in that particular area of management.

After the checklist has been completed, a panel of judges—normally including the senior management and the manager's direct superior—evaluates each of the statements on a seven- or eleven-point scale. The points given by each of the judges are then averaged and their standard deviation calculated. If the deviation of any of the statements is large, it means that the judges have widely different opinions; and, as a result, the statement is eliminated from the checklist. The average value calculated for each of the statements is then taken as the weighted average.

The evaluator is then given a copy of the final checklist, but without the weights assigned to the statements. The task of the evaluator is to indicate whether each manager does or does not engage in the behavior indicated by the statements on the checklist. Once the checklist is completed by the evaluator, weights are assigned to the positive statements, and the weights for each checklist totalled.

Quantitative Methods

Here, the evaluator can compare individual performance with absolute standards either on a conventional rating basis or by using behaviorally anchored rating scales. Although the latter technique sounds rather formidable, it simply means that the evaluator is given specific examples of managerial behavior which serve to "anchor" each point on a rating scale. Such examples can go a long way toward reducing the ambiguities that result from using a conventional rating scale. How does one develop specific examples of behavior? By utilizing the judgments and opinions of experienced managers.

Each of the absolute standards techniques has its own particular advantages. The critical incidents method provides a certain degree of feedback to the manager being appraised; the evaluator with the checklist of critical incidents can discuss each statement with the manager, thereby reducing the possibility of disagreement. The weighted checklist method tries to avoid halo error on the part of the evaluator (for example, leniency, strictness, and so on) by not assigning weights to the statements when the checklist is given to the evaluator. This procedure reduces the possibility of inter-individual errors.

The fact that both the critical incidents and the weighted checklist methods employ only carefully selected, valid statements of the appraisees' performances make them very attractive approaches. Also, these methods provide clear differentiation between successful and unsuccessful performance, while conventional rating methods do not.

As for the behaviorally anchored rating scale, there is a distinct advantage in that the method concentrates mainly on behavior and performance, rather than on personality. Furthermore, when using this scale, there is almost always high inter-rater agreement.

The quantitative methods, like all other methods, have certain drawbacks. For example, the quantitative methods require a great deal of time and effort before they can be successfully implemented. This time and effort may be difficult to justify unless large numbers of managers are involved, and for this reason the methods are used widely only in large organizations. On top of this, the statements or scales must be continuously updated and validated to ensure that the behaviors specified are still relevant to the job and predictive of performance.

DIRECT INDEX

In this method, managers are evaluated solely by the results they have achieved. This method differs in several respects from the comparative procedures and absolute standards approaches. The most obvious difference is that information about managerial performance can be obtained more directly, without being filtered through an evaluation process.

Direct index, as it is commonly used, includes a measure of performance appropriate for each manager's role: productivity (for production managers), financial standing (financial managers), manpower utilization (personnel managers), and turnover or sales (marketing managers).

If the performance of a production manager is to be evaluated, then the direct index used is the improvement of productivity or the output of plants. This, however, is related to the type of machines used, the types of production processes, and also the proper and efficient utilization of workers and materials, without regard to the cost.

When appraising the performance of financial managers, the index used includes the overall improvement in the company's financial standing—for example, liquidity, debt to total asset ratio, and debt collection. As for the marketing manager, the index is usually sales, profit, and market share. This should reflect the efficient use of both sales personnel and marketing mix variables: price, promotion, product development, and distribution.

The chief advantage of the direct index method is that it eliminates constant error, such as bias and leniency, since the role of the appraiser is disregarded. For that matter, variable error due to disagreement among judges (a problem found in the absolute standards method) is also eliminated.

Nevertheless, direct index does not always give a clear indication of managerial performance. Under certain circumstances, outcomes are not clearly defined and, therefore, not directly attributable to the manager being appraised. Clearly, in such circumstances, direct index is of little value.

THE FIELD REVIEW TECHNIQUE

As its name suggests, this technique requires that representatives (usually from the personnel department) go out into the "field"—that is, other departments—to gather information about the work of various managers. The approach is used mainly with lower level managers.

The technique works like this: The representatives, usually equipped with standardized questionnaires, hold interviews with the immediate superiors of the managers being appraised. Questions are asked and answered informally. The managers are then assessed and the results are typed out along with the recommendations of the personnel department representatives. After the assessment sheets have been typed, they are sent back to the respective evaluators for any corrections they may have.

One advantage of the field review approach is that the answers are carefully analyzed. If it is discovered that a manager is being consistently judged unsatisfactory, then the analyst will attempt to find reasons for the low rating. Possible remedial programs may then be suggested.

To be effective, the informal interviews should be held three or four times a year, and this leads to still another advantage. Evaluators tend to pay more attention to the activities of the managers.

However, there are certain limitations. The need for regular, fairly frequent interviews can easily strain the resources of the personnel department. If the department is inadequately staffed—a problem with many smaller firms—it may not even be possible to carry out such interviews on a regular basis. On top of this, the interviews are likely to be subject to the bias and/or leniency of the evaluator.

FEEDBACK OF APPRAISAL INTERVIEW

This basic approach can be broken down into three distinct methods: the tell-and-listen method; tell-and-sell; and the problem-solving technique.

Tell-and-Listen

The aim here is to encourage the manager to air personal feelings about the evaluation. The interview is usually conducted in two parts. The first part is concerned with the evaluation process, in which the manager is informed of his or her strengths and weaknesses and any remedial measures that may be necessary. In the second part, the manager is encouraged to express honest feelings about the evaluation. The evaluator then assumes the role of a judge, listening to objections and trying to refute those objections.

If the interview is handled correctly, it not only serves as a feedback process, but also as a means whereby the frustrations and negative feelings of the manager can be relieved or siphoned off. However, this involves much skill and experience on the part of the appraiser.

The greatest benefit to be gained from tell-and-listen is that it ensures a good relationship between evaluator and manager. The manager is left with a positive attitude towards the evaluator and the company as a whole. The disadvantage? Simply that the manager may not get to know where he or she stands or, indeed, how to improve performance.

Overall, tell-and-listen encourages a greater amount of upward communication than is normally the case (which, by the way, is also one of the inherent advantages of the problem-solving approach). The method also provides both the evaluator and the manager an opportunity to learn more, since experiences and views of both parties are pooled. Finally, the method helps remove resistance to change, and thus stimulates changes. Too many changes, however, may make it impossible for managers to function effectively.

Tell-and-Sell

This method aims to inform managers of their evaluation just as accurately as possible. In essence, the evaluator tells the manager how he or she is doing, gets the manager to accept the evaluation plans, and finally, to follow the plan outlined for improvement. Considerable skill in handling the interview is essential if this technique is to be a success. The interviewer must be able to persuade the manager to change in a prescribed manner; the use of monetary incentive bonuses is not uncommon.

Tell-and-sell is usually highly effective when the manager is inexperienced, insecure, and needs assurance from authoritative figures. Also, suggestions of respected superiors tend to be more acceptable to managers of the lower and middle ranks. Even so, lengthy interviews are usually necessary in order to convince these managers—if they can be convinced. If a manager remains unconvinced, even after lengthy discussions, then he or she may feel that personal interests are incompatible with the company's—a feeling that can lead finally to withdrawal.

Still, the greatest danger here is when the middle-level manager agrees with everything that has been said. When this occurs, it usually means that the manager's thinking and interest has not been stimulated; instead, the manager has been led into trying to please the appraiser.

The Problem-Solving Approach

Unlike the first two feedback of appraisal methods, this approach involves the interviewer as a helper rather than a judge. What the interviewer is trying to do in this technique is help the manager improve his or her job performance. The interviewer urges the manager to describe the difficulties he or she is encountering, responds to those comments, and, in general, coaches the manager through a short course in self-examination. It's critical, however, that the suggestions for improvement come from the manager—not the interviewer. The interviewer's role is to stimulate, not to influence.

PERFORMANCE STATISTICS

The desire to substitute quantitative and qualitative measures for conventional rating methods has led to the development of appraisal techniques using performance statistics. The techniques developed include profit performance (budget) measurement, performance standards, and (of course) management by objectives.

Profit Performance Measurement

Profit performance measurements are widely used for the appraisal of divisional managers' performances. This is especially true when the division is treated as a profit center of an investment center. In order to have a sound appraisal system,* it is necessary to:

1. *Mark off profit centers correctly.* Indeed, it is often necessary to segregate service centers from profit centers. The reason for this

---

*These guidelines are suggested by J. Dean, "Profit Performance Measurement of Divisional Managers," in *Performance Appraisal*, ed. Whistler, T.L. and Harper, S.F. (New York: Holt, Rinehart and Winston, 1962).

is simple enough: Managers can be held responsible only for their own profit center. In marking off profit centers, it's important to ensure that each center has operational independence, access to alternative sources and markets, and separable costs and revenues.
2. *Establish economically sound intracompany transfer prices and business arrangements.* The prices of goods and services sold to other divisions should be negotiated at arm's length by profit center managers. If difficulties arise in the pricing of goods, then market price should be used.
3. *Measure the contribution profits of the profit center correctly.* A correct measurement of the profit contribution of the division is essential. In order to be fair and realistic, current profitability, growth, and progress (in the technological sense) must be considered, too.
4. *Determine realistic standards of contribution profit performance.*
5. *Establish incentives.* These can take the form of executive compensation and various nonmonetary rewards that will induce profit center managers to do what is best for the organization as a whole.

Since profits are affected by a combination of many factors, it is impossible to set standards for each profit center with certainty. Instead, we must to some extent rely on subjective judgment in setting annual profit objectives.

In addition, in attempting to establish a sound profit objective, it is essential that the economic climate and the competitive situation be predicted as accurately as possible. However, even this particular strategy can occasionally fail. The profit objective may be sound at the start of the period, but changes in either economic climate or competitive situation may make it impossible to achieve set objectives.

Another disadvantage is that although the performance of divisional managers is usually evaluated once a year, a longer period of time is needed for investment in equipment and other assets to yield profits. Because of this, it is advisable to carry out both short- and long-term performance appraisals, with due credit given to long-term earnings.

The Appraisal of Managerial Performance—33

Performance Standard Method

Here, specific standards are set jointly by the appraiser and the manager at the beginning of the appraisal period. In setting up these joint standards, the evaluator must make the manager aware of the goals and objectives of the organization. Once the standards for the job are set, the manager is held responsible for achieving the end results, which are then compared with the set standards. It is important to draw up the standards carefully, so that they are neither too difficult to achieve, nor too easy. It is also a good idea to put the standards in writing so that there will be no question as to exactly what is expected of the manager.

Performance can be measured in very simple terms: achievement of the standards is considered "acceptable"; failure to achieve is "not acceptable." However, it is probably good policy to refine the measurement somewhat, so that managers will have some idea of where they stand even if they fail to achieve the set standards. For example:

A very good performance
B good performance
C average performance
D below average performance
F poor performance

At the end of the appraisal period, the appraiser and the manager meet again to compare performance with the set standards. Standards that are viewed as important are given more weight, and standards that have been met well are rewarded. In situations where the manager's performance is below average or poor, he or she is encouraged to give reasons for the failure and to cooperate with the superior in seeking appropriate remedies. Finally, new standards and objectives are established for the next period, based on the results of the appraisal just completed.

There are many advantages in using this particular method. First, the method is useful because it includes several basic elements of managing: planning, review, and direction. Second, there is little room for bias or leniency on the part of the appraiser; nor do personality and appearance influence judgment—the only important factor is results (or performance). Third, the method serves as an excellent communication device, with common understanding existing between appraiser and manager. Finally, the method gives managers a good idea of their performance at the end of the appraisal period. Furthermore, they can check on their performance whenever they wish, since they know what standards they are expected to meet.

One disadvantage of this method lies in the fact that setting the standards is by no means an easy task. Knowledge and experience are both essential prerequisites. Another weakness is that performance is reviewed only once a year. In a sense, this deprives managers of the opportunity to succeed, because the method is essentially a post-mortem of actions completed, rather than a guide to better performance. However, this weakness can be easily remedied by reviewing performance more frequently.

Management by Objectives

In essence, this approach is almost the same as the performance standard method. It is result-oriented, with due attention focused on the achievement of long-term corporate goals as the end result. Long-term objectives are essential since they help guide managers toward the achievement of shorter term goals, while in the long run achieving the long-term objectives, too.

The main difference between MBO and performance standards are: (1) MBO requires that both quantitative and qualitative objectives be set, while performance standards does not; (2) MBO requires that performance objectives be set for each level of the organization and that all the objectives be closely interrelated.

Including both quantitative and qualitative objectives in the evaluation process simply means that managers' responsibilities must include those that can be *measured* (for example, sales, production, output, and so on) and those that must be *judged* (the introduction of new training programs, the development of new processes, and so on).

The second difference noted above is a little more complex. When appraisers meet with appraisees (managers) to set up objectives, the standards by which the achievement of the objectives is measured are also jointly set. These appraisees—who are themselves upper level managers—in turn set up objectives (both quantitative and qualitative) for their own subordinate managers (middle level), thereby dismantling the objectives into parts. These "parts" are assigned to each middle-level manager in accordance with his or her ability and accountability. Since the setting and splitting of objectives continues until the lowest level of management is reached, the end result is that the objectives set for each level of the organization are closely interrelated.

As in the case with the performance standards method, appraisal is carried out once a year. In MBO, however, each manager checks on the performance of his or her subordinates periodically to ensure that they are performing in accordance with whatever pace has been set. Needless to say, it is essential that superiors set their subordinates on the right track when employing this method.

The main criticism of MBO is that there is usually a problem of setting optimum standards. In addition, it is difficult to use a system of rewards in MBO because goals are set for each individual separately. There is always the danger that subordinates will set goals that are relatively easy to achieve—to the detriment of the overall corporate goal. It should also be noted that some managers criticize MBO because they feel it is primarily a management development device rather than an evaluative tool.

4

Utility as a Measure of Performance

The general problem of appraising managerial performance involves three stages:

Stage I Setting up quantifiable, observable measures of performance along key dimensions and recording the manager's performance along these dimensions for an appropriate time period.

Stage II Assigning corporate utilities to these levels of performance so that performances along different key dimensions can be added.

Stage III Comparing the total corporate utility generated by a manager with those generated by other managers in comparable situations.

Stage I presents no great difficulties and has already been dealt with in this monograph.

Stage II—the assigning of utilities seen by the appraiser as representative of the organization—is a more difficult task. For example, utilities are widely held to be ordinal rather than cardinal, so the addition of utilities from different sources raises problems. If utilities were cardinal—and it should be noted that we often speak of utilities as if they were cardinal; in fact, we even have a conceptual unit (the Util.)—then it would be theoretically possible to adopt a linear planning approach relating the utility produced along various dimensions to the resources available. A feasible area could then be mapped out and the worth of a manager's performance determined by sensitivity analysis. At an informal, intuitive level, of course, this is done all the time.

Another approach could be the use of a conjoint measure matrix. We can illustrate this, for two measures of performance, by using as an example a factory that transports the dangerous chemical Acrotonitrile to customers. (An underlying assumption here is that the number of people exposed to danger when the chemical is moved through urban areas is 20 times greater when it is moved by rail than when it is moved by barge.) This can be proxied by the time it takes to transport a load one mile—or its reciprocal, speed. The other measure is safety, and this can be proxied by ton-miles moved per hundred dollars insurance. There is a trade-off between safety and transportation speed by train (10 to 30 m.p.h.) or barge (4 m.p.h.)

Conceptually, a utility matrix could be developed along conjoint measurement lines, as shown in Exhibit 5.

As can be seen, the utility of a combined performance measure of moving a ton of Acrotonitrile one mile at 30 m.p.h. and a medium degree of safety would have a utility rating of 15.6. This is superior to a

Exhibit 5. A conceptual utility matrix.

		\multicolumn{4}{c}{Speed M.P.H.}
		4	10	20	30
		(1.5)	(2.5)	(8.4)	(12.4)
Safety	300 miles (9.8)	11.3	12.3	18.2	22.2
(Ton-Miles	200 miles (3.2)	4.7	5.7	11.6	15.6
per $100 of insurance)	100 miles (1.6)	3.1	4.1	10.6	14.0

(Utilities per ton-mile)

Exhibit 6. A two-dimensional measure of performance using indifference curves.

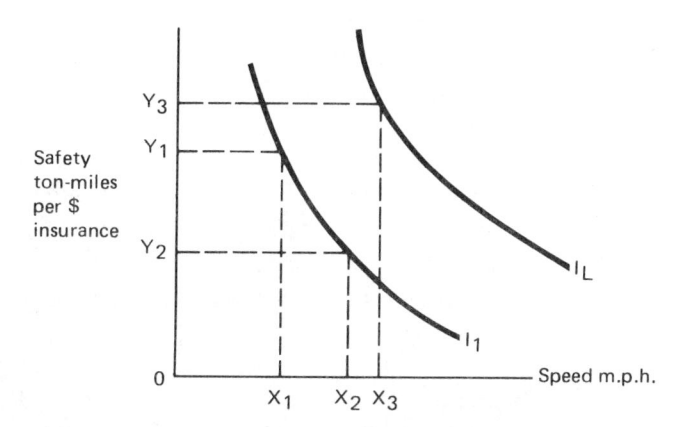

Safety ton-miles per $ insurance (vertical axis with Y_3, Y_1, Y_2); horizontal axis: Speed m.p.h. with X_1, X_2, X_3. Curves labeled I_L and I_1.

combined performance of moving it at 10 m.p.h. with a high degree of safety, which has a utility rating of 12.3.*

The problem is the assumption that utilities are cardinal, which is dubious. This assumption can be relaxed if we use an indifference curve approach. Although the utilities of collections of goods are extremely difficult to quantify in a cardinal sense, it is possible, by using what is known as a revealed preference technique, to identify a range of different collections of goods that for an individual have the same total utility.

If only two goods are involved, the various combinations that give rise to a particular level of utility can be plotted on a two-dimensional graph, thus forming an indifference curve. For goods, a three-dimensional indifference surface could be constructed. Indifference curves and surfaces lying farther out from the origin represent higher levels of utility (see Exhibit 6). This can be applied to a combination of measures of managerial performance.

Using Exhibit 6, we can see that transporting Acrotonitrile at speed OX_1 and safety level OY_1, and transporting at speed OX_2 and degree of safety OY_2 would have the same combined utility. Transporting it at

*The data on moving Acrotonitrile are from a report on the Joint Conference of the Eno Foundation, published in *Traffic Quarterly* (April 1980).

speed OX_3 and with a degree of safety OY_3 would be on a higher indifference curve and would represent a higher level of utility compared ordinally with the other combinations. *The technique can be applied to multidimensional combinations of measures of managerial performance and can be used to rank ordinally composite performances along multiple dimensions.*

In practice, what appraisers do at an intuitive level is conceive of groups of sets of combined performances of equal utility within the group, with each group having a different utility from the other groups. They form an indifference map, the appraiser being indifferent between performance sets in a particular group. For example, using only three criteria, output, cost, and quality:

		Units	Cost per Unit	Fail Rate (Percent)
	Set A1	20,000	$3.00	1.0
	Set A2	18,000	$2.85	.9
Group A	Set A3	17,000	$3.10	.5
	⋮			
	Set An			
	Set B1	20,000	$2.95	.95
	Set B2	18,000	$2.80	.85
Group B	Set B3	17,000	$3.00	.45
	⋮			
	Set Bn			
Group N	Set Nn			

What the above tells an appraiser is that the sets of performances in Group B represent a higher level of utility than those in Group A; accordingly, the appraiser will prefer any set of performance in Group B to any set in Group A. What it does not tell the appraiser is whether a Group B performance is outstanding or merely average. It only says that a Group B performance is better than a Group A performance.

The rating on a level of performance depends not only on the utility of the performance, but also on the resources with which it was

Exhibit 7. Production possibility curves along performance dimensions.

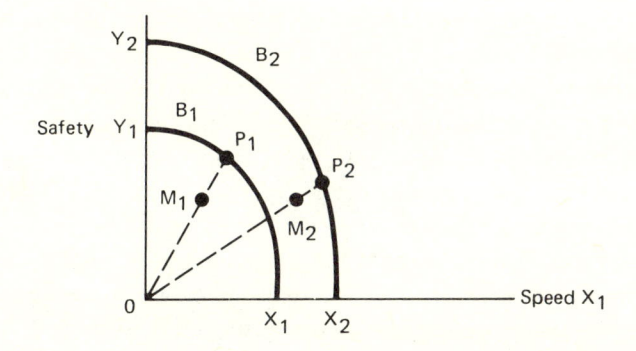

achieved. This is equivalent to Stage III of the appraisal process. It involves comparing the performance with those achieved by other managers with different resources working along the same dimensions (although giving them different weightings).

Another possible technique switches from indifference curve analysis to a production possibility curve approach—from ordinal utility to cardinal outputs along performance dimensions incorporating desired mixes of objectives.

In Exhibit 7, the axes are outputs of certain goods, suitably quantified with a given budget of resources B_1. A manager M_1 has the choice of spending the budget on various combinations of goods. (For the sake of consistency, we will continue to assume that the two goods are safety and speed.) The manager could spend the entire budget producing units of safety with a maximum possibility of OY_1; or the entire budget on speed with a maximum possibility of units OX_1; or on producing various combinations of speed and safety lying along the production possibility curve B_1.

Another manager (M_2) has a larger budget (B_2), and his or her maximum performances lie along Production Possibility Curve B_2. Given human fallibility, neither manager actually produces a maximum possible performance; nevertheless, their performances are marked on the graph as M_1 and M_2, with their maximum performances given their individual weightings of the desirability of speed and safety, which are P_1 and P_2. The merits of their performances are in the ratios:

The Appraisal of Managerial Performance—41

$$\frac{\text{Achieved Performance}}{\text{Possible Performance}} \quad \frac{OM_1}{OP_1} \quad \text{or} \quad \text{and} \quad \frac{OM_2}{OP_2}$$

With experience, a sense of the merits of particular multiple combinations of performances, given particular inputs of resources, will be built up. These can be used to apply labels—Outstanding, Good Barely Satisfactory—to the various groups of combined performances that are collected.

In practice, of course, because an infinite number of combinations of performance are possible, only a very limited collection of combinations at a few levels—Outstanding, Good, Acceptable, Unsatisfactory, Disastrous—are computed for various levels of resource input. Then the composite performances of particular managers controlling particular sets of resources are matched against specimen performances to give the ratings of the managerial performances.

Stated formally, the computational difficulties are daunting, but the process is a model of the intuitive rule-of-thumb way conscientious appraisers go about their business. And, it should be noted, the approach is not without some theoretical respectability.

5

Appraisal in Functional, Divisional, and Matrix Organizations

There are basically three types of organization in industry today: functional, divisional, and matrix organizations. Each type has developed out of the need for more sophisticated structure to cope with the increasing communication overload brought on by increases in size.

For the most part, organizations reduce the overload either by decentralizing into smaller divisions or by instituting lateral relations that cut across vertical lines of authority, thereby creating a matrix type of structure. However, no matter which method is used, the performance of managers still needs to be evaluated. Most of the approaches to appraisal used by the three organizational types have already been discussed.

Although it would simplify matters considerably if all appraisal methods worked equally well in each of the three types of organization, this unfortunately is not the case. Some methods work better in a functional organization, others in a divisional organization, and still others in a matrix organization. To make matters even more complicated, the methods differ for top- and middle-level managers in each type of

Exhibit 8. Types of organization and levels of management.

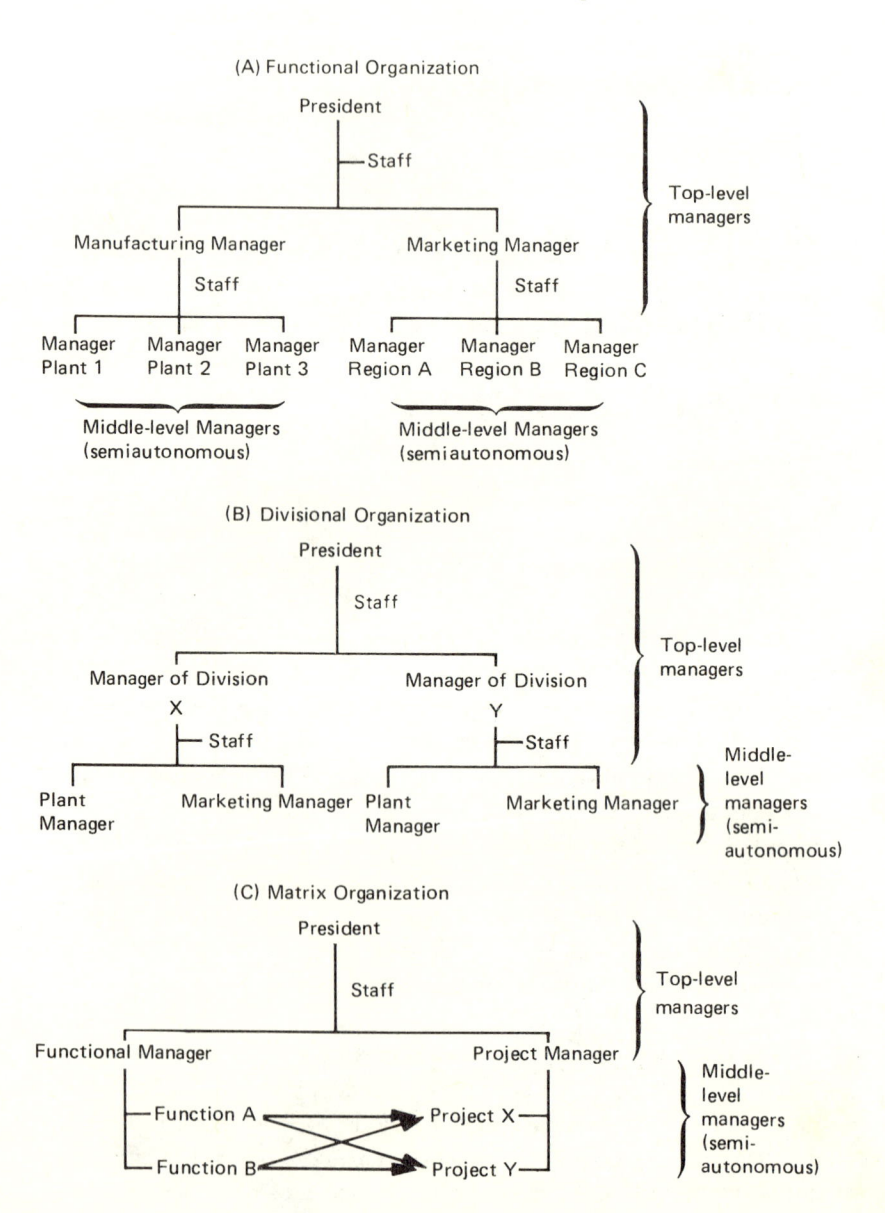

(A) Functional Organization

```
                        President
                           |—Staff
         ┌─────────────────┴─────────────────┐
   Manufacturing Manager              Marketing Manager
         |—Staff                            |—Staff
   ┌─────┼─────┐                      ┌─────┼─────┐
Manager Manager Manager         Manager Manager Manager
Plant 1 Plant 2 Plant 3         Region A Region B Region C
```

Top-level managers (President, Manufacturing Manager, Marketing Manager)

Middle-level Managers (semiautonomous) — Plant Managers

Middle-level Managers (semiautonomous) — Region Managers

(B) Divisional Organization

```
                  President
                     |—Staff
         ┌───────────┴───────────┐
  Manager of Division     Manager of Division
         X                       Y
         |—Staff                 |—Staff
    ┌────┴────┐             ┌────┴────┐
  Plant   Marketing       Plant    Marketing
 Manager   Manager       Manager    Manager
```

Top-level managers

Middle-level managers (semi-autonomous)

(C) Matrix Organization

```
                  President
                     |—Staff
         ┌───────────┴───────────┐
  Functional Manager        Project Manager
    |—Function A ──────→ Project X—|
    |—Function B ──────→ Project Y—|
                  (crossed arrows)
```

Top-level managers

Middle-level managers (semi-autonomous)

44—AMA Management Briefing

organization. Top-level managers are directors, divisional heads, project managers, and functional managers. Middle-level managers (which also include lower-level managers and supervisors) are plant managers, regional managers, marketing managers, and personnel on a similar level of authority. The two levels of manager for each type of organization are shown in Exhibit 8.

Functional organizations. These organizations are structured in such a way that each manager is held responsible for a specific function. The operation of the organization as a whole is usually coordinated by the president (or, possibly, the general manager), because he or she is the only individual with an overall view of the business. This means that responsibility for earning profits cannot be assigned to individual managers.

The various appraisal methods suitable for functional organizations are shown in Exhibit 9.

Divisional organizations. In these organizations, each division is treated either as a separate entity or as an independent profit center, under the direction and control of a divisional head. Since divisional

Exhibit 9. Methods suitable for appraising managerial performance in functional organizations.

Methods of Performance Appraisal		Top Level Managers	Middle Level (Semiautonomous) Managers
Feedback of appraisal interview	Tell-and-listen	X	X
	Tell-and-sell		X
	Problem-solving approach	X	X
Performance statistics methods	MBO	X	X
	Profit performance		
	Performance standard	X	X
Absolute standards	Quantitative		X
	Qualitative		X
Comparative procedure	Ranking technique		
	Forced distribution		
Direct index	—	X	X
Field review technique	—		

The Appraisal of Managerial Performance—45

Exhibit 10. Methods suitable for appraising managerial performance in divisional organizations.

Methods of Performance Appraisal		Top Level Managers	Middle Level (Semiautonomous) Managers
Feedback of appraisal interview	Tell-and-listen		X
	Tell-and-sell		X
	Problem-solving approach		X
Performance statistics methods	MBO	X	X
	Profit performance	X	
	Performance standards	X	X
Absolute standards	Quantitative		X
	Qualitative		X
Comparative procedure	Ranking technique		
	Forced distribution method		
Direct index	—		X
Field review technique	—		X

managers report directly to the president, divisional organizations tend to be more straightforward than functional organizations, as far as the management control and appraisal process is concerned. However, each division is itself a functional unit, but on a smaller scale.

Exhibit 10 shows the suitable appraisal methods for divisional organizations.

Matrix organizations. In these organizations, responsibilities are arranged by function; superimposed on this structure is another structure where responsibilities are arranged by project. Projects are carried out under the direction of project managers, with personnel, material, and ancillary services needed for these projects under the responsibility of functional managers. The main problem in this type of organization is management control and the appraisal of managerial performance.

In this type of organization, project and functional managers are assumed to be top-level managers, while executives who work under them are assumed to be second-level managers. It should be noted that project managers' jobs are not determined with much certainty, since

Exhibit 11. Methods suitable for appraising managerial performance in matrix organizations.

Methods of Performance Appraisal		Project Managers	Functional Managers	Middle Level (Semiautonomous) Managers
Feedback of appraisal interview	Tell-and-listen	X	X	X
	Tell-and-sell			X
	Problem-solving approach	X	X	X
Performance statistics methods	MBO		X	
	Profit performance			
	Performance standards		X	
Absolute standards	Qualitative	X	X	X
	Quantitative	X	X	X
Comparative procedures	Ranking technique	X		X
	Forced distribution method			X
Direct index	—	X	X	X
Field review technique	—			X

this depends very much on the plans or objectives of the organization as a whole. Furthermore, project managers' jobs also depend on whatever project the company may happen to have. As for functional managers, their responsibilities are somewhat fixed, and include supplying needed manpower, recruiting and training new personnel, and allocating such resources as material and funds.

The methods of appraising managers' performances in matrix organizations are shown in Exhibit 11.

The Appraisal of Managerial Performance—47

6

Issues Arising from Current Appraisal Practices

A typical managerial appraisal procedure, as followed by a number of progressive companies, might go something like this:

Stage I Job definition and analysis is at least partly done by the appraisee, but with the agreement of his or her superior. This stage covers duties, authority, and responsibilities.

Stage II The expected key results are identified, and the terms for their measurement are developed. These key results are typically defined by the superior in line with the overall corporate plan, but with the appraisee able to make representations if the results are unreasonable or unattainable. The considerations in this stage take into account the available resources and an acceptable arrangement on the relationship between allocated resources and expected results.

Stage III The quantifiable performance is computed at the end of the period, and the more qualitative aspects assessed by the appraiser.

Stage IV An appraisal interview is held after the measurement of performance. At the interview, the appraisee has the opportunity to discuss his or her performance, explain any special problems and/or difficulties, review his or her strengths and weaknesses, and talk about future plans for development.

THE APPRAISAL FORM

A typical appraisal form might ask for an assessment of the manager's performance, and possibly request a statement regarding his or her preset targets. In general, the questions are openended. The space allowed for answers can vary from one or two lines to several paragraphs.

Typically, an overall grading of performance—ranging from outstanding to inadequate—would be part of the appraisal form. Provision can, of course, be made for longer, more detailed descriptions of the rating. Generally, there are sections for assessments of potential and recommendations for promotion, transfer, and further personal development.

There is sometimes a space for comments after the appraisal interview. Finally, as a rule, the forms are countersigned, with comments as necessary by a superior of the person doing the evaluation.

THE APPRAISAL INTERVIEW

A formal appraisal interview is not obligatory; however, most firms include them as part of the assessment process. Nor is there any hard-and-fast rule as to how many people should be present at an appraisal interview. A great many interviews involve only the appraiser and the manager, but in many cases the appraiser's superior is also present. There are, in fact, some instances where top-level management—a divisional general manager, for example—also sit in on the interview.

Opinion is divided on the desirability of more than one appraiser being present at the interview. To some extent, it depends on the purpose of the interview. If the purpose is to complete and refine the assessment of past performance, then a second judge might well make for a fairer assessment. And if the purpose is to discuss career prospects, then a high-ranking manager might be in a position to give more authoritative answers. Indeed, the main argument in favor of the presence of a high-ranking second appraiser is making sure that recommendations are carried out.

On the other hand, if the purpose is to motivate the appraisee, then the presence of a high-ranking executive might inhibit matters, particularly if the executive is a stranger to the appraisee.

The presence of a high-ranking third party can also interfere with the normal processes of assessment and counseling. Consider a situation where a middle-level manager (A) is being interviewed by his or her immediate superior (B), while the divisional manager (C) is present. Is B being assessed by C as he or she grapples with a difficult situation? Does A direct all of the answers to C in the hope that he or she will impress the top person? And will A be receptive to counseling from B in such a situation? From this point of view at least, it would seem that the presence of a high-ranking second appraiser does more harm than good.

LENIENCY OF APPRAISERS

A common complaint is that in almost all industrial rating schemes the average mark awarded is above the midpoint of the rating scale. This apparent reluctance to use the whole scale may be seen as evidence of evasiveness on the part of the appraisers. It depends on what rating scales are used. The means of the distribution of absolute levels of performance of managers must coincide with the midpoint of another scale measuring the suitabilities of managers.

Nevertheless, a tendency toward leniency does seem to exist. This may stem from an appraiser's reluctance to damage a junior colleague's career prospects; the manager being appraised is usually given the benefit of the doubt in marginal cases. Also, where ratings have to be revealed, some managers almost certainly show excessive leniency simply to avoid unpleasantness.

If individual appraisers were consistent in the degree of leniency they showed, it would present little difficulty. Firms could always make statistical adjustments to allow for different degrees of leniency by different managers; as a matter of fact, some firms have done just that. Unfortunately, though, many managers are not consistent. They are overly lenient on one occasion, less so on the next.

All in all, it seems that leniency is a function of a number of variables: age (slightly positive correlation with leniency); psychological distance— for example, the number of subordinates under an appraiser (negative correlation); and training in appraisal (negative correlation).

VALIDITY

Validity means to what degree a procedure actually measures what it is supposed to measure. Generally, it is unlikely that a multipurpose procedure would have a high degree of validity in all of its aspects. In addition, many appraisal schemes do not prescribe techniques, but ask for answers to such questions as, "Is he promotable?", and leave the methods of arriving at the answers to the respondents. In such cases, of of course, the validity of the scheme depends on the quality of the respondents.

A crude measure of the overall validity of schemes involving appraisals of large numbers of executives is to plot the distributions of ratings on the various dimensions. If the curves obtained differ significantly from normal distribution curves, then the validity can be considered suspect. (It should be noted that to do this, the scales must be arranged so as to encourage the respondents to use all points on the scale, rather than only the upper grades to avoid labeling their subordinates as unsatisfactory.)

If acceptable psychological tests are available, they could be used to check the validity of a scheme regarding particular attributes such as intelligence, extraversion, introversion, and aggression. And in the case of individual managers, follow-up studies could indicate the validity of earlier appraisals.

But the most sensible safeguard against invalid schemes is the continual assessment of the relevance of the criteria, the freedom from deficiency (that is, things being left out that should be considered), and freedom from contamination (that is, the inclusion of things that should be left out).

One way of improving the validity of multipurpose procedures is to introduce a separate procedure for each purpose. There is general agreement that the salary-fixing function should be kept separate from the performance improvement/motivation function. It has also been suggested that there are three functions to be dealt with separately: salary administration, management potential, and performance improvement.

EFFECTIVENESS

Effectiveness refers to the efficiency of the once-a-year appraisal in motivating managers to better performances. It is difficult to believe that the knowledge that there is a formal annual day of reckoning will not eliminate some slackness, but the only way to be sure is to carry out a controlled experiment.

H. H. Meyer, E. Kay, and J. R. R. French reported such an experiment at General Electric in connection with appraisal interviews.* They found, among other things, that criticism has a negative effect, while praise had little effect one way or another. Defensiveness resulting from critical appraisal produced inferior performances. Coaching should be a day-to-day, not a year-to-year, activity.

They arrived at the conclusion that comprehensive annual performance appraisals are of questionable value. Their evidence can possibly be interpreted as showing that having been subjected to the psychological pressure of an impending appraisal, and having under that pressure improved their performance, "men" are unmoved by praise that they know they deserve and resent criticism that they feel is unjust. That coaching should be a day-to-day business, rather than an annual activity, seems self-evident. It implies that more appraisal, not less, is required.

*"Split Roles in Performance Appraisal," *Harvard Business Review*, January/February 1965.

7

Appraisal of Performance and Effectiveness

The aim of every business enterprise is to obtain certain objectives, which may or may not be explicitly stated. The degree and manner of achieving these objectives reflects the effectiveness of the enterprise. Effectiveness should be appraised regularly, of course, so that management can take action designed to improve any facet of the enterprise that is slipping in its overall level of performance.

The concepts of *business effectiveness* and *business efficiency* are often confused—or are erroneously assumed to be identical. It is important to distinguish between the two concepts. Effectiveness is concerned with the degree to which the company goals are achieved. Efficiency is concerned with how well resources are used in any of the company's operations, regardless of whether the operations contribute to the achievement of the company's goals. In other words, efficiency is concerned with doing things right, while effectiveness is concerned with doing the right things. Efficiency can usually be measured by the productivity of the resources used, while effectiveness, in general, requires more complex measurements.

Since business enterprises tend to be complex organizations, they usually have multiple objectives that cover every aspect of the enterprise's activities. Thus, the determinants of business effectiveness are numerous, and include economic, financial, technical, ecological, and social factors. In order to assess the overall effectiveness of a business, it is necessary to consider all factors and their individual effectiveness. High levels of overall effectiveness can be obtained only if all the subsystems are equally effective.

Because the factors that determine overall effectiveness are varied, it follows that the criteria and techniques used for measurement also need to be varied. While various financial models have been examined earlier in this monograph, it is important to look also into the organizational social criteria that might affect managerial performance.

There are a number of criteria that can be used to measure the performance of an organization's social system: the organization's ability to attract and retain skilled managers, the extent of harmonious interpersonal relationships and interdepartmental relationships, the extent of utilization of high-level manpower, the degree of perception of organizational goals by management, and the readiness of the organization to respond to changes in its product-market environment.

One study* uses regression analysis to show that social effectiveness is positively and highly correlated with each of three variables: managerial attitudes, processes, and practices. The most important of the three is managerial attitudes. The study suggests that these three variables can serve as surrogate measures for organizational social performances.

HUMAN RESOURCES

A high business performance requires the effective use of all the enterprise's resources. This includes its human resources—especially managers and skilled workers in whom the company has invested time and money to provide adequate training.

Another aspect of human resource management is ensuring that enough expertise is available to meet future needs. How effective a firm

*S. B. Prasad, "A Construct of Organizational Social Effectiveness" *Management International Review*, Vol. 13 (1973), pp. 4-5.

is, in this respect, can be measured if there are some detailed estimates of manpower requirements. An effective manpower planning model might show the transitions of manpower between levels within the firm, the number of employees who leave the firm, and the number of entrants required at each level. Recruitment requirements could then be compared with actual recruitment to assess whether the enterprise is effective in manpower planning.

SOCIAL OBJECTIVES

The measures of managerial performance appraisal considered so far have been used to assess to what degree the economic and financial objectives of the firm were being achieved. But modern businesses often have broad social objectives as well. These objectives are rarely defined in quantifiable terms, and performance appraisal in this area is comparatively underdeveloped.

The First National Bank of Minneapolis used a technique called "the social indicator approach" to measure the effectiveness with which it was achieving its social objectives. Ten aspects of the quality of life were selected, and quantitative measurements were developed for each one. Those indicators were then used to compare the performance in the social programs. This approach has also been used by a New York bank in conjunction with branch performance statistics.

Another approach to measuring social objectives performance was pioneered by Abt Associates, a New York City based firm of consultants. Their approach—called the constituent impact approach—uses a balance sheet format to record all the interrelationships between a company and its various constituencies; that is, employees, neighbors, and so on. The transactions are essential social costs and benefits. However, this method is too complex to be applied to large organizations.

The Bank of America developed a social management program approach in which the basis of assessing performance is data from an internal managerial information scheme. The program aimed at improving performance by examining and comparing the performances of different existing schemes.

8

Summary

All techniques for appraising managerial performances have their strengths and limitations. Consequently, one key for truly effective appraisal is to use the techniques selectively and with discrimination. This means understanding why certain techniques do not work well in certain environments—and exploiting the strengths of those techniques that *do* provide useful measurements. Note, for example, that MBO is still relatively unpopular, in spite of the extensive literature advocating its use. Apparently, the difficulty stems from problems in identifying and agreeing on measurable behavioral objectives. The truth of the matter is that in certain situations the objectives are virtually impossible to identify in behavioral terms.

Other techniques have their limitations as well. They work with a narrow view of management, or they are subject to bias, or they are influenced by personality rather than performance. What is most popular? According to a recent survey, those methods using rating scales, such as discussed in Chapter 3 under "absolute standards."

One thing seems clear: Even though formal appraisal programs are in existence in most organizations, appraisers usually receive very little formal training. One consequence is that they tend to use techniques that are popular, comfortable to apply, or "traditional" within a particular organization. Little thought is given to the total usefulness of the effort.

The three stages for managerial performance outlined at the beginning of Chapter 4 provide a general, but essential, framework. Within this framework, a successful appraisal program should meet these criteria:*

1. The method of appraisal should attempt to appraise a measurable organizational objective. The program used must be able to measure performance against preselected, verifiable goals.
2. The method should be operational; that is, it must take into account what is being done and how the various jobs are being carried out.
3. The method of appraisal should be objective; that is, it must be verifiable so that it is possible to determine whether these goals have been accomplished.
4. The method should be participative; that is, it must be accepted by those being appraised. This is why participation by both appraiser and appraisee in jointly considering the program is of the utmost importance.
5. The method should be constructive; that is, it should be aimed at improving the abilities and performance of the managers being appraised. It should be able to point out mistakes and weaknesses and provide learning experiences.

Essentially, the aim is to appraise past managerial performance and to provide the groundwork for ongoing improvement—in the manager's present job. If one wants to go one step further and also look at promotability, there is no reason this can't be done at the same time. But assessing a manager's promotability is different from assessing the person's ability in his or her present job. Failure to realize this often results in managers being promoted to the point where they become clearly inefficient.

Since past performance is an inadequate guide to promotability, relevant personal qualities need to be assessed—qualitatively and subjectively if need be, although psychological tests might be of use. This assessment should be a preliminary stage in a manager's development. Further steps should include the planning of developmental experiences with built-in quantitative objectives designed to provide more

*H. Koontz, *Appraising Managers as Managers* (New York: McGraw-Hill, 1971).

The Appraisal of Managerial Performance—57

substantial evidence of a manager's suitability and potential.

In functional organizations, because of the particular structure of the organization, the responsibility for earning profits—and, indeed, for any other organizational development—cannot be assigned to specific top-level or middle-level managers. As a result, the methods of appraising their performance are somewhat more important than in other types of organizations. In divisional organizations, responsibility is at least clear-cut, which makes it possible to use only a few methods of appraising the performance of divisional heads.

However, in matrix organizations, where the performance of one manager (a project manager, for example) is very much dependent on the performance, attitude, and cooperation of another (functional) manager, it becomes difficult to hold an individual manager responsible for a specific task. Furthermore, because of the variety of projects undertaken, it is often not feasible to use MBO, profit performance measurement, or even the performance standard method to appraise performance. Why? For the simple reason that neither standards nor objectives can be set with reasonable certainty. In short, only when the projects or jobs are known in advance can objectives and standards be set for managers and organizations.

Bibliography

Anthony, R. N. and Dearden, J. *Management Control Systems.* Homewood, Illinois: Richard D. Irwin, Inc., 1976.

Bittel, L. R. *The Nine Master Keys of Management.* New York: McGraw-Hill Book Company, 1972.

Cummings, L. L. and Schwab, D. P. *Performance in Organizations: Determinants and Appraisal.* Glenview, Illinois: Scott, Foresman & Company, 1973.

Drucker, P. F. *Management: Tasks, Responsibilities, Practices.* Heinemann, 1974.

Haeri, S. "Performance Appraisal: What Managers Think." *B. I. M. Information Summary No. 136,* 1968.

Kahalas, H. and Leninger, W. E. "A Manpower Planning Model for Organizational Effectiveness." *Long Range Planning,* Volume 8, No. 4, August 1975, pp. 11-14.

Kelly, P. R. "Reappraisal of Appraisals." *Harvard Business Review,* July/August 1958, pp. 59-68.

Locher, A. H. and Teel, K. S. "Performance Appraisal—A Survey of Current Practices." *Personnel Journal,* May 1977, pp. 245-247.

Mahler, W. R. and Freizer, G. "Appraisal of Executive Performance: The 'Achilles' Heel' of Executive Development." *Personnel,* Volume 31, 1955, pp. 429-441.

McGregor, D. "An Uneasy Look at Performance Appraisal." *Harvard Business Review,* May/June 1957, pp. 89-93.

Meyer, H. H., Kay, E. and French, J. R. R. "Split Roles in Performance Appraisal." *Harvard Business Review,* January/February 1965, pp. 123-129.

Patton, A. "How to Appraise Executive Performance." *Harvard Business Review*, January/February 1960, pp. 63-70.

Prasad, S. B. "A Construct of Organizational Social Effectiveness." *Management International Review*, Volume 13, 1973, pp. 4-5.

Reeser, C. "Executive Performance Appraisal—The View from the Top." *Personnel Journal*, January 1975, pp. 42-46.

Rock, M. L. and Lewis, L. M. "Appraising Managerial Performance." *Handbook of Business Administration*, H. B. Maynard, ed., New York, 1967, pp. 480-488.

Rowe, K. H. "An Appraisal of Appraisals." *The Journal of Management Studies*, March 1964, pp. 1-25.

Solomons, D. *Divisional Performance, Measurement and Control.* Homewood, Illinois: Richard D. Irwin, Inc., 1968.

Stewart, V. and Stewart, A. *Practical Performance Appraisal.* Farnborough, England: Gower Press, 1977.

Whisler, T. L. and Harper, S. F. *Performance Appraisal.* New York: Holt, Rinehart and Winston, 1962.

Yoshino, M. Y. *Japan's Managerial System: Tradition and Innovation.* Boston: Allyn and Bacon, Inc., 1967.

Monmouth County Park System
Library